Oxford Read and Imagine

Beginner

I'm Sorry

By Paul Shipton
Illustrated by Steve Cox
Activities by Hannah Fish

Contents

Hello!
My name is Rosie.
Hello!
My name is Ben.

This is Grandpa.
Hello!
Now let's read this story, I'm Sorry.

'Let's go to the park!' says Grandpa.

'We can ride the bikes!' says Ben.

'Clunk, you can ride this bike,' says Rosie.

Clunk can't ride the bike.

He hits a tree!

'I'm sorry,' says Clunk.

I'm sorry.

Go to page 15 for activities.

They walk to the park.
Grandpa sits down and the children play.
'Catch this, Clunk!' shouts Ben.
Catch this, Clunk!

Clunk runs.

Then he falls over.

'I'm sorry,' says
the robot.

Clunk is sad.

→ Go to page 16 for activities.

There is a little cat in the park.

Ben likes cats. 'Hello, little cat,' he says.

Rosie kicks a ball to Clunk.

'Can you kick it to me?' says Rosie.

‘Yes! Yes, I can!’ says Clunk.
Clunk kicks the ball.
It does not go to Rosie.

Go to page 17 for activities.

The cat is scared.
It runs up a tree. It runs up and up.
'Oh no!' says Ben. 'Look! The cat can't climb down!'
Oh no!

Grandpa looks at the cat.

'I'm sorry,' he says. 'I can't climb trees. Clunk can help you.'

Go to page 18 for activities.

'Can you climb trees, Clunk?' asks Rosie.

'No,' says Clunk. 'I can jump. Look!'

Clunk jumps up to the cat.

The robot has the cat in his arms.
The children are happy.
The cat is happy.
And Clunk is happy, too.

Go to page 19 for activities.

Activities before you read

Talk **Look at the front cover of this book. Answer the questions and talk to a friend.**

1 What can you see?

2 How many children are there?

3 Where are they?

4 Do you have a bike?

1 Match.

Activities for pages 4–5

1 Write the words.

1 ride

d e r i

2 ________

r e t e

3 ________

k e i b

4 ________

r k a p

2 Write *yes* or *no*.

1 Grandpa says, 'Let's go to the school.' no

2 Rosie has a bike. ________

3 Clunk hits a car. ________

4 Clunk says, 'I'm sorry.' ________

Talk **Can you ride a bike? Talk to a friend.**

Activities for pages 6–7

1 Choose and write the correct words.

Grandpa, Clunk, and the children [1] walk to the park. Grandpa sits down and the children play. Ben [2] ____________ to Clunk. Clunk [3] ____________ and falls over. Clunk says, 'I'm sorry'. The robot is [4] ____________.

runs

~~walk~~

happy

sad

shouts

2 Match.

1 They walk	and falls over.
2 Grandpa sits	'Catch this, Clunk!'
3 Ben shouts,	sad.
4 Clunk runs	down.
5 Clunk is	to the park.

Activities for pages 8–9

1 Match.

- 1 kick
- 2 cat
- 3 ball
- 4 park

2 Order the words.

1 park. / is / There / a little cat / the / in

There is a little cat in the park.

2 kicks / a ball / Rosie / to / Clunk.

3 the / Clunk / ball. / kicks

4 ball / Rosie. / The / doesn't / go to

Talk **Do you like cats? Talk to a friend.**

Activities for pages 10–11

1 Look at the picture on pages 10 and 11. Write *yes* or *no*.

1 The cat is up a tree. ______

2 The cat is scared. ______

3 Clunk is up a tree. ______

4 Grandpa has a ball. ______

5 Ben is kicking the ball. ______

2 Circle the correct words.

1 The cat runs **up** / **down** a tree.

2 The cat **can** / **can't** climb down.

3 Grandpa **shouts** / **looks** at the cat.

4 Grandpa can't climb **trees** / **robots**.

5 Clunk can **fall over** / **help**.

Activities for pages 12–13

1 Put a tick (✓) or a cross (X) in the box.

1 This is a robot. 

2 This is a cat. ☐

3 This is a park. 

4 This is a tree. 

2 Look at the picture on page 13. Answer the questions.

1 How many children are there? two

2 Where is the cat? in Clunk's ____________

3 Is the cat happy? ____________

4 Is Grandpa sad? ____________

Talk **Do you like this story? Talk to a friend.**

Project

What happens?

1 Match.

Grandpa

Rosie

the cat

Ben

the children

Clunk

- kicks a ball to Clunk
- sits down
- play
- jumps up to the cat
- says 'Hello, little cat.'
- runs and falls over
- runs up a tree
- kicks the ball
- looks at the cat

2 **Now complete the sentences with words from activity 1.**

In the park, Grandpa [1] sits down and the children [2] ________. Clunk runs and [3] ________ ________! There's a cat in the park. Ben says 'Hello, little [4] ________.' Rosie kicks a ball to [5] ________. Clunk [6] ________ the ball. The cat is scared. The cat [7] ________ up a tree. Grandpa [8] ________ at the cat. He says, 'Clunk can help you.' Clunk [9] ________ up to the cat! They are happy.

3 **Draw your favorite picture from this story.**

Talk **Talk to a friend about your picture.**

Picture Dictionary

arms

ball

cat

catch

climb

down

fall over

happy

help

jump

kick

park

ride

robot

run

sad

scared

shout

tree

up

Oxford Read and Imagine

Oxford Read and Imagine graded readers are at eight levels (Starter, Beginner, and Levels 1 to 6) for students from age 4 and older. They offer great stories to read and enjoy.

Activities provide Cambridge Young Learner Exams preparation. See Key below.

At Levels 1 to 6, every storybook reader links to an **Oxford Read and Discover** non-fiction reader, giving students a chance to find out more about the world around them, and an opportunity for Content and Language Integrated Learning (CLIL).

For more information about **Read and Imagine**, and for Teacher's Notes, go to www.oup.com/elt/teacher/readandimagine

For a free Audio download of the story in a choice of American and British English, go to www.oup.com/elt/readandimagine

Activity supports Cambridge Young Learner Starters Exam preparation

OXFORD
UNIVERSITY PRESS

Great Clarendon Street, Oxford, OX2 6DP, United Kingdom

Oxford University Press is a department of the University of Oxford.It furthers the University's objective of excellence in research, scholarship, and education by publishing worldwide. Oxford is a registered trade mark of Oxford University Press in the UK and in certain other countries

First published in 2014
2026
22

ISBN: 978 0 19 472224 7

Printed in China

ACKNOWLEDGEMENTS

Main illustrations by: Steve Cox.

Activity illustrations by: Dusan Pavlic/Beehive Illustration; Alan Rowe; Mark Ruffle.